Brown Skin with Three Ponytails

A journey towards forgiving, while never forgetting

By

Promises McClain

Table of Contents

Acknowledgements

This book came about due partly to my desire to make sure that my children understand who I was when the day comes that I can no longer speak for myself.

To my beautiful children, Ashley, Lyndsey and Leonard, Jr. Thank you for being the best children a mother could ever ask for. I appreciate your love and admiration. I thank God for choosing me to be your mother.

To my mother, whom I have learned to love unconditionally; at a distance. I thank you for raising me in the church and for allowing me to stay home from school when the bullying became too much for me to bear. I also thank you for inadvertently teaching me to be a leader in spite of all that goes on around me. Thanks for telling me, "You're pretty you'll see," when I would look in the mirror and all that I could see were bumps on top of bumps and thick glasses on my face. I release all the hurt but most importantly; I forgive you.

I want to thank all of my surrogate mothers: Jacqueline Battle, Yvette Ginyard and Marilyn Jarrette for your love, guidance, encouragement and support. For as you know, my journey has been mottled with many days of agonizing emotional pains, days of crying endless rivers of tears, excruciating worries and extreme levels of stress and anxiety. I thank you (my friends) first for your much needed guidance, for your listening ear, but most importantly for providing me with motherly love, hugs and kisses when God knew I was in dire need. I've made many strides in spite of the many circumstances that arose at various times in my life and I needed the touch or support of a mother to help me not only find way my but to light the path so that I could see my way through. I love you.

To my lifelong friends, Tabitha Wright, Kenya Townsend, Denita Binion, Tomeka Howell, Chartis Ingraham, Rotunda Caldwell-Gorman, Sharon Hilton, Bryant Jones, Joelle Roy and Erin Wassel, who have stood by me even when they didn't understand and/or agree with the many "flavors" of Gina. I appreciate and love you endlessly. Thank you for listening to me, for your hugs (even if it had to be through a phone); Thank you for allowing my tears to flow, for not thinking I was crazy, as I described the craziness that was going on around me but most of all thank you for your unconditional love and true friendship.

To my unmentioned Connecticut Kings and Queens, thank for great memories and providing me with a place to truly call my home. To my Georgia Peach Divas and Gentlemen, I thank you for telling me that I am tall and beautiful and that everything was going to be okay. To my sweet spirited and supportive editor Mrs. Franchesca Lane-Warren, The editing nerd, who listened to me cry as I explained my vision in writing this book, you understood and supported my vision; Thank you. To Dr. Jerry Jones and Dexter Thompson, I also thank you.

To Tamara Green and Hadiyah Johnson, I thank you for the encouragement to forge on and obtain my Master's degree because you felt "I was a good worker and smart." You never know how even the smallest positive thoughts and words said to a person can change that person's life forever.

To Avion Speed, although we're not biological related, you are and will always my family. You have embraced me and all my imperfections and I love you forever for that. Our relationship has provided me authentic feelings of affection, while giving me strength when I've been weak, access to a much needed constant "voice of reason", and a smile. Your honesty in my worst moments has saved my life and I appreciate just being able to call you family. I love you.

To Keer Hardison, thank you for sharing your journey through times of great struggle while allowing me to share mines. You understood and validated my feelings of tremendous hurt behind rejection. Through you I found my strength to forge on.. But most importantly I appreciate you for loving me unconditionally and for embracing me as a part of your family. I love you.

To my cousin Yvonne Savage, you both returned to my life at a time when I'd just about given up on the notion that I could be a part of my birthright. Your voice, your smile, your laugh gave me hope that it can get better and not to give up on the word and meaning of family...I love you.

To the many therapists and counselors (both formal and informal) who helped me when I was in crisis. I thank you for helping me maintain my mind, my soul, my spirit because the devil was definitely busy.

To the many young women and men who've crossed my professional path, thank you for sharing your stories of survival, your tears of hurt, pain and/or shame, your innocence in the mist of your wrongdoings and your victories in the end. You trusted me with your most painful moments but most importantly I thank God for placing you in my path. I will NEVER GIVE UP ON YOU.

Finally, to my dear sweet sister, Tammy, you are my rock. I thank you for always opening your heart and allowing me in. Your honest dialogue and your openness has allowed me to walk strongly before you. You have given me credit when you've felt it due (that means more to me than you'll ever know). You showed me patience, until I get could get it right. Most importantly you have leaned on the side of love, by encouraging me, for accepting my love and for never turning your back on me. Most importantly for allowing me to be, that of which I didn't ask to be...your eldest sister...I love you dearly.

Beginning at a very young age, I endured multiple abrupt, bond damaging separations from my family. Being raised by my mother a (undiagnosed) clinically depressed, single (yet married) woman; who would instill seeds of hate, dishonor and distrust to her children for many years, all masked by her warped religion. It would take years for me to find myself amid all the drama.

Further complicating my adolescent development was the sporadic and chaotic encounters with the man who by birthright I called my father. My father was a bipolar, black male who would never be able to support me or my siblings financially and/or emotionally. However, we'd been taught by our mother to love him and that our love for him is unconditional. She did that because she was protecting us from the realities she lived with daily. She choose to endure years of an emotionally and psychologically draining marital relationship.

My mother would eventually divorce our father only to marry a sadistically, cunning, Muslim man, who briefly professed to be a Christian as a way of swooning my mother into his arms after impregnating her out of wedlock. Mr. Abdul did not make any effort to get to know myself and/or my siblings on a personal level prior to their marriage. Mr. Abdul's militant and cold hearted hate for her children would eventually severely damage my relationship with my mother. The main disciplinary measure he used during their marriage was kicking her teenage children out and not allowing any communication with the unit family. My mother's hopes were that he'd make her "family" whole but what she failed to realize was the value of what she had-her own family. As my mother was on a quest to provide her girls with a "stable home life" along with a real "father figure" all enmeshed in her religiosity; her decision would prove to be the final straw for my relationship with her, as it would significantly damage our mother daughter bond for many years.

Looking back over my life, I can say this life has given me lots of lemons but I'm in the process of making some awesome lemon aide. Once this book is published, my hope and desire is that this book reaches people who endured similar challenges as me and that everyone is able to see how God brought me through my storm. For He is the reason I still stand.

Chapter 1: THE SLAP

My mother ran into my room and began snatching, ripping and tearing up ALL the pictures of my boyfriend off of my wall as she yelled, "IF YOU DON'T LIKE MY HUSBAND YOU CAN'T PUT THIS UP!" I remained silent but began trying to grab the pictures before she got to them; however, this seemed to make her become even angrier. She then began to scream repeatedly at me, "GET OUT, GET OUT!!!"

I tried to grab a few of my things but as I would pick up my various personal items she'd rip them from my hands. So I grabbed the only thing she could not tear from me and that was my pillow. Then unexpectantly, SHE SLAPPED ME. As my face turned back towards her, it seemed like everything STOPPED and we were now in slow motion as tears began to stream slowly down my face. I looked into my mother's eyes knowing that the slap was about to change the life I'd known before it, and that its effects would be forever.

I continued to look at my mother, then at her new husband, Mr. Abdul, and then at my sisters; my heart hurt as it beat swiftly- I finally spoke these words with confidence and sincerity, "I'm leaving and I'm NEVER coming back." At that moment everything instantly returned to fast pace mode. I stopped trying to grab things but held on to my pillow, and I began to move out of the door of my bedroom heading towards the top of the stairs. Realizing I was actually going to leave, my mother went completely wild. She began swinging her fists hitting me all about my arms and back. As her fists landed on my back, she got angrier and began to sink her nails in my skin. This was all while her husband, Mr. Abdul, made passive attempts to hold her back. She continued to scream, "GET OUT, GET OUT, GET OUT," as she was hitting me.

I eventually managed to make it past everyone, jumping down two and three steps heading out the front door. As I reached the bottom of the stairs, I looked back and up the stairs to take one last look at each of my sister's faces; Megan, Lauren, then Sunni (she was tiny) and then I continued to make my way out the door.

It was dark and chilly outside as I walked down the hill crying first softly then hysterically. I finally ran into a family friend, Tony. He asked me, "What's wrong Dee?" He noticed I was crying and carrying a pillow. I told him, "My mother kicked me out and I'm not going back". Tony said, "Well go to my house; my mother is home." He walked me to his house and his mother, Patricia, came down the stairs quickly after hearing all the commotion. Still clutching my pillow, I told her, "My mother kicked me out and I'm NEVER going back," as I continued to cry. I was just 19 years old but on that day I also became a homeless, church girl about to be thrust out into the unfamiliar world without the covering and blessings of my mother. This is my story; about a young girl's struggle to survive in a world that is so cold.

Chapter 2: I DIDN'T ASK TO BE THE OLDEST SISTER...

The earliest memories of my life are when we lived in a two bedroom apartment in a family oriented public housing project in Stamford, Connecticut. Our apartment was modest but still included a living room, kitchen, two bedrooms and single bathroom for your average happy family of five to share. Our bedroom was located on the second floor of our apartment and at that time my sister, Megan, and I shared a full size bed. While my sister, Lauren, had a single twin bed been but as my other siblings came along they'd first be placed in the crib located in my mother's tiny room. Later, as the children continued coming, my mother would replace that furniture with two bunk beds and two large dressers for our room.

I slept on the bottom bunk and was given the two top drawers (out of four), half of the top of the dresser and an end table to put my belongings. We all managed to share one closet which was also located in our bedroom; everyone had a section within which to put their clothing. As you can imagine, we learned the necessity of sharing very early.

We were a very poor, yet loving church going family. Privacy was unheard of in our home. If anyone was using the bathroom to only pee, we knew it was normal for one or two of our siblings to come in the bathroom to brush their hair or to get something they needed; as being at that time we were all girls. It became a normal routine for us to form a sort of a stair step formation in the bathroom mirror as we got dressed for school in the mornings. So, of course me being the oldest and tallest, I would always stand in the back, then Megan and then Lauren so everyone could see themselves in mirror.

Our home felt safe, was immaculately clean, fresh and calm in spite of our mother's almost back to back childbirths. In order of births, there was me, Megan, Lauren, Sunni, Naveh and A.D. Our brother she would have with Mr. Abdul.

From as far back as I can remember I can hear my mother saying, "Danni you're the oldest!" Most times she'd be yelling this affirmation at the top of her lungs, while other times she'd utilize the friendly, yet constant reminder tone. This statement grew into not only a way for her to chastise me for my faults, but for the faults of my siblings. Ultimately, my mother felt, they did whatever they were doing to cause them to get into trouble because I wasn't watching them or worst because they were emulating me. Sadly, she would never note anything positive that I'd done that they may have emulated, which always made me feel worthless and insecure.

At first, being the oldest was just because of my birth order, but as additional siblings were born, being the oldest began to weigh heavily on my life, my soul, and my being (to be honest, it still does at times). If my siblings fell while playing, of course, it was my fault; if they talked on the phone too late, it was my fault. If they talked back to our mother she would say, "You see she got THAT from you." If they pouted it was my fault; if they got into trouble at school it was my fault. The short sentence, "It's your fault," began to haunt me.

It was so tough for me, I could literally be in bed sleeping, not at home or not have even demonstrated the negative behavior of my siblings; yet our Mother would still always find a way to proclaim that all troubles that arose within our family was somehow my fault. As one could imagine, living under that type of scrutiny and criticism would take a toll on my emotions, my mind and my spirit. I became a very nervous child and found it hard to trust that of which many treasure...my family.

Cleaning, cooking, childcare, discipline and most importantly, maintaining order, was my job because as aforementioned, if anything went wrong within our family it would be my fault.

I can remember one, hot sunny day in Connecticut when I was about 9 years old, being outside playing without a care in the world. We were running, jumping, skipping and flipping over the bars in the public housing project where we lived. I was watching my 6 year old little sister, Megan. She was behind me doing what she always did...trying to keep up; making attempts to do everything I'd done. Although I loved my little sister, I still wanted to be able to play carefree, with my friends and without the difficult responsibilities of watching her, as I was a child too.

On this particular day, Megan was trying to emulate my ability to flip over the bars but she slipped coming around the bar and fell, hitting her head on the cement steps. I ran to try to help her but was immediately horrified as I watched blood gush through her skin onto her forehead. Megan was screaming hysterically as she too felt the pain, but more so looked horrified when she saw the amount of blood.

Although I was upset because she was hurt and bleeding, my knees almost buckled as I thought about being blamed for causing her injury. I knew would I be held accountable because I was responsible for her when she was in my care. We walked home quickly with Megan screaming all the way, and hearing all the commotion, our mother met us at the door yelling, "WHAT HAPPENED!!!???"

She quickly noticed the blood gushing from Megan's head and hurriedly grabbed a towel, placing it on my sister's head, while simultaneously scooping her up as she ran out the door saying she was on her way to the hospital. I exhaled as I thought to myself, "Thank God our mother was handling the situation." I was still scared since I didn't know the extent of Megan's injuries, but I did know she was bleeding badly.

They were gone for a few hours but when they came back, my mother brushed by me, went up the stairs and placed my sister in her bed. Our mother's bed was a place of refuge we ONLY got to go to when we were sick. Noting the hostility from my mother, I waited for a few minutes trying to build up the courage to go upstairs to see how my sister was doing. I'd been so worried; however, as I got to the top of the steps my mother yelled at me with great contempt, "LOOK what you did!!!" Then came the words that grew to haunt me throughout a large part of my life..."IT'S ALL YOUR FAULT!! If YOU hadn't been out there running and jumping she wouldn't have ran, jumped and hurt herself. You know she's going to do what you do! You weren't watching her!"

Those words pierced my heart. I was devastated, hurt, and overwhelmed by my mother's hostile remarks. I still managed to glance over at my sister who'd heard my mother's conviction. Megan was lying in our mother's bed with a large bandage across the top of her forehead, slightly stained with blood, with a few protruding stitches peeking through the bandage.

Megan looked like she had been in a great deal of pain but medication seemed to be soothing her. Our eyes met; she was calm but I sensed she too agreed with what our mother was saying about her pain being my fault. My heart sank; as I looked at both my mother and my sister, I thought to myself, "Had they forgotten that I was just a kid too?" The agony wasn't over for me as I also sensed that my sister was somehow happy and she felt that I deserved to be punished. Occasions like this birthed severe sibling rivalry, envy, jealousy and incessant discord between us. In the end my mother chose sides instead of acknowledging the fact that we were BOTH children and there was no ill will involved in this accident; as it was an accident.

My other sister, Lauren, was a liar and very mean spirited. She was my mother's original "baby girl". Lauren became more resentful and mean when our other siblings eventually came along. She felt they took her title of "THE BABY" that our mother had drilled into our heads. While growing up my mother constantly forced us to make provisions for Lauren by saying, "You know she's the baby, help her. She's the baby, give it to her, etc". I remember on one occasion when we lived on 142 Connecticut Street, we were all under the age of 12 and our mother went out and left us home alone; of course, I was in charge. Being playful kids, we decided to pull a mattress off of one of our beds and we all began to jump on the mattress.

We were all happily jumping, throwing each other down and doing flips on the mattress, when we realized our mother was pulling up to our apartment. We quickly put the mattress back just prior to her stepping in the door as we made a pact not to tell Mommy. As our mother walked in the door, Lauren, with her unquenchable appetite for attention, ran to our mother to get her hugs and kisses and then did the unthinkable—she broke our pact. I watched her eyes as she grabbed my mother's ear and told her that Megan and I had been jumping on the mattress. We were devastated; not only by the betrayal but by the fact that Lauren failed to tell our mother that she too had been jumping on the mattress. So our mother immediately went to get her comb, gave us a long lecture complete with scriptures to explain the necessity of spanking, spare the rod spoil the child, honor your parent and then Megan and I got a spanking; while Lauren lay on my mother's shoulder watching.

Something in me changed that day towards Lauren. I swore as long as it was in my power I'd never to allow her to put me in a situation in which I would be blamed for something she did and/or took part in. I started avoiding and/or limiting our interactions especially if we had to be alone, because if anything wrong happened or if she got hurt I might as well get the comb myself. Although I still loved Lauren, I became more on guard and cautious in her presence because I knew she couldn't be trusted.

The pressure from being the oldest child wore hard on me. Looking back, I feel like I never had a childhood. I always felt like the weight of the world lay on my shoulders. As a child, my mother would constantly drill into me and my siblings' head that I was responsible for everyone, which translated into, I would be held accountable for any and everything that went wrong regardless of who may have contributed to the particular incident. I believe this mentality made it hard for me and my siblings to develop a bond. Instead it deepened the already sowed roots of distrust, envy and strife between my siblings and I.

As I went through my adolescence, I naturally became interested in obtaining more freedom and an independent identity. I no longer wanted the weight of the invisible badge of reverse honor, which hung around my neck called, "Danni you are the oldest sister," or the heavy cross of burden that wheeled, "Danni it's all your fault".   This manifested in my desire to be able to go to parties at the Brickenwood Center like my peers; to go outside and hang with my friends by myself; to go to "sinner's," aka non- born Christians- homes but most importantly NOT to be held responsible for my siblings. Well of course, I would never be allowed to go to a Brickenwood Center party, but I was eventually allowed to go to some sinners' homes but that's only because my mother thought their parent was an upstanding citizen overall. The only time I would be allowed to go places without my siblings was if it were a church sponsored event and/or road trip.

Chapter 3: A STARCH, A VEGETABLE AND A MEAT

I'm not sure exactly when, where or why she left us, but my mother stopped parenting us during the latter part of my elementary school years. For as long as I can remember I've been responsible for my siblings, but now I was responsible for more demanding tasks such as preparing dinner and cleaning the entire house. I had to make sure all of my siblings ate a balanced meal that included a starch, a vegetable and a meat (a meal usually prepared by an adult or a mother). My siblings would often complain about my cooking and say it was nasty and they didn't want to eat it. However, I was just a kid too so at times those comments actually hurt my feelings but I had no other choice, as it was my responsibility to cook balanced meals for my siblings and I. So with little too no direction, I did the best I could. Always making sure the meal included a starch, a vegetable and a meat; all while our mother either lay in bed sleeping, reading the bible or on the phone talking to her family.

I was also in charge of delegating chores, as well as ensuring that they were done, but more importantly done correctly. Interestingly enough, I feel my sisters resented me for the role of "The Enforcer" to this day. What they never realized is this role was not a desired role but presented to me with an "or else I'd be disciplined" clause. To this day, there is an intense hostility between my siblings and I that on occasion "rears its ugly head" during arguments. I'd often wondered to myself, "Do they know I didn't really want to lead but I had too?" As children, the only time we would hear from our mother other than preparation for a religious affair, was when a ball dropped, which is bound to happen when you leave a child in charge of children.

Saturday was deemed the "total house cleaning day" in our home. We had to wash walls down with bleach and comet;. We had to: clean the bathroom, vacuum all rugs, sweep the stairs down, clean out the refrigerator, etc. To make matters worse, all of this cleaning had to be done QUIETLY because if anyone so much as got the giggles, and it awoke our mother before noon, we would all get popped with the comb. Our cleaning routine was rigorous; if my mother happened to awake from one of her naps early to get a glass of Pepsi and observed even a speck of debris on her glass, she'd immediately push ALL the dishes back into the sink for us to re-wash. To this day my friends and some family are annoyed at my obsession with cleanliness but what they don't understand is that my childhood job was to ensure that our home was clean and cleaned right! I can even remember being awakened out of my sleep if the kitchen wasn't properly cleaned.

At one point in my early childhood, my mother was addicted to Pepsi Cola. She'd even laugh thinking about how much she loved it. This was a horrible situation for us because if she happened to run out of Pepsi, she'd make us walk all the way to the A & P supermarket where it was priced less. The A& P supermarket was located over 2 miles roundtrip, away from our apartment. She eventually began to add on other grocery items which eventually lead to us being sent to the A&P with a complete grocery list.

The hardest part about this arrangement was we'd have to carry heavy bags back home. We'd stop several times along the way because we'd grow tired of carrying those heavy bags. In addition, I hated when she made me purchase her feminine products from the store. I was young so I had to build up the nerve to pick up those types of items. I felt like the whole store stopped to watch me pick up sanitary napkins; that they knew something very personal about me (I had my period). We'd eventually find a way to make our torturous roundtrips fun. During our trips to the A& P we began to walk a little out of our way to different residential neighborhoods. We loved one particular house because they had a cement driveway on a hill.   So we'd put all the bags down at the top of their driveway and walk in a straight line playing as if we were a train. We would march up and down this driveway making sounds of a train. Interestingly, those homeowners never came out to tell us to get off their property; probably because they saw we weren't being destructive and were just having fun.

Chapter 4: THE LOVE OFFERING KIDS

My mother spent most of my childhood sleeping, or laying in bed watching TV; only getting up for church activities. Our week usually went like this: Monday night, consecration, Tuesday night, choir rehearsal, Wednesday night, bible study, Thursday, teen night, Friday night, evening service and Saturday was noon day prayer. This was all after having begun our week with Sunday morning and evening services.

Our mother was a single, yet married, woman attending a ministry that taught women that they should pray for their healing of their dysfunctional marital relationship indefinitely, or that's the way in which my mother absorbed the word. We spent many hours in church and our mother NEVER thought to pack snacks for us so our stomachs would be growling during the long day and evening services. We would sit for hours; eventually laying on our growling stomachs but being held back from complaining by threats of being popped by our mother's comb.

Interestingly enough, I would grow to love church because it was better than sitting at home and doing nothing. Even if we were on punishment, attending church was an activity we never missed and eventually a place that I grew to love going to.

From time to time Mary, a church member, would bring clothing and toys for my siblings and I, and my mother would always take the "mess" and thank her with a "fake" smile, as she walked out of our door. My mother would then quickly turn towards us, giggling, as she hushed us, sheepishly throwing the items in the garbage. As we grew older, she seemed to get joy from recognizing the potential humiliation her children may have to endure due to being continuous recipients of love offerings by Mary.

To make matters worse, we didn't even look in the bags from Mary, as her bags were always filled with used or torn clothing, along with a few broken toys, BUT because my mother was always the first in line for a handout, she didn't want anyone to think we weren't constantly grateful. Besides, we were the love offering kids. Our very financial survival was dependent upon love offerings so even if we couldn't use the majority of the items we were given, we had to maintain a posture of incessant gratitude kind of like slaves opening their mouths to smile for potential owners.

Unwavering gratitude pierces the very essence of a love offering, as it is supposed to leave a person feeling loved and supported as that is supposed to be the feeling of the needy. Since my mother was never able to maintain a job to support her very large family on her own, requesting love offerings would become her method of obtaining rationings for her children. As she continued to receive these handouts we were often left feeling disgraced, as it was a constant souvenir of just how poor we really were. Our very survival was solely dependent upon the genuine kindness of another person's heart.

I remember it was Friday night service and devotion had just concluded; it was time for TESTIMONIES! My sisters and I sat back watching, as people who felt BOLD enough to share what the LORD had done for them took the microphone to speak. One by one, they told stories about how God had blessed them saved them or showed them favor and these testimonies kept going. To us kids it was all very interesting as time and time again people would become emotional as they shared their struggles and ultimate victories as God was so good.

As I sat there I often thought to myself, "Oh how I'd love to get up to tell a story that caused people to get excited about how GOOD GOD is." But those stories never came to me, as a child, as I never saw the victory in the life we lived. All of a sudden Mary, one of the church members who would bring us love offerings, got up to take the microphone. Immediately, she caught our attention as she was known to say and do strange things. So we expected whatever she had to say would be funny and interesting. We watched intently as she sashayed her way up to the stage. Mary was a preteen who was very innocently sexy; she had hips, breast and a killer waist. I'm sure many female adult members silently HATED this about her while the men...well let's just leave that alone. As she began to speak we braced ourselves; as the giggles were on the attack!!

As she walked up to the microphone, she began to tear up causing everyone to sit forward in their seats. She began to whisper softly into the microphone as she needed to contain her emotions. Ever so softly she said, "I'd like to thank God for blessing me, taking care of me." She then paused to clear her throat, "and for allowing me to be able to give Sister Danielle's kids clothing." We were immediately embarrassed but more importantly offended as we wrestled with relentless thoughts of how we could instantly inflict bodily harm upon Mary, as a means to relieve all the aforementioned emotions. BUT when you didn't think it could get worst, the Pastor was so moved by her testimony, (they love when young people tell stories of how God blessed them), that he requested that WE stood up, to be seen and to allow them to clap for the charitable spirit of Mary.

At first we didn't budge; we were hoping God would swoop down and scoop us up out of this madness, but our beloved mother motioned with the "OR ELSE" face, for US to get up, per their request as we were the love offering kids. My first thought (as a non-receiving member of her love offering) was that "Mary had never given ME a damn thing! Why should I get up"? I was older and much bigger than Mary and I could not fit any of the clothes she brought but as quickly as I thought that, I thought about my sisters and how they must be feeling so I gave in and we all stood up. Everyone in the church clapped and clapped, hugging Mary as she smiled wildly, remaining completely oblivious to our torment, as she felt she'd done a good thing. She, of course, never knew the clothing she'd given to us would never be worn, let alone taken out of the bag, because at the end of the day we were the love offering kids so that fact didn't matter.

Chapter 5: EARLIEST MEMORIES OF MY MOTHER

I have no knowledge of my mother's journey towards her decision to becoming a devout Christian. Her Christianity, periodic devotional lead, and daily activities primarily involved attending church functions because church was HER LIFE- literally! When my mother wasn't sleeping, she was either sitting on her bed reading the bible or on the phone with a friend or family member from the church or on her way to church. Her bible and notebooks filled with notes from sermons were always lying beside her in bed. Her bible was her faithful husband, constant companion and the answer to all her problems. The only males I can remember coming in our house that wasn't her brothers was my father or a few young men from the church, or a boy from the neighborhood. I can only remember seeing my father in my mother's bedroom once, although he'd father 5 of her children. It was almost like she didn't want us to see him in her bed, or for us to think that they were ever together intimately because that would be a sin and send a bad message for her girls; yet he remained her husband for 16 years.

My mother always had scriptures posted on her headboard and refrigerator. All her friends (and the majority of our family) were involved in our church and/or were Christians. My mother didn't trust non- believers and made sure we as children knew they weren't to be trusted because "they were sinners". Furthermore, anyone who wasn't attending our church- to our mother, their Christianity was questionable, because the ministry they'd chosen wasn't ours.
Thus, they weren't being taught the truth.

She loved all the new urban Christian musicians, singers and song writers. My mother, a singer herself, desperately longed for me and my siblings to perform as a gospel singing group. Although we all loved to sing we did not all share her passion for singing. In our home there was always the latest gospel music blaring through our apartment day and night. Because the music had urban edginess, we as little girls would dance around in our panties happily singing to the music with our mother and hitting all those key notes.

She eventually made a way for her girls to perform together for our church. This arrangement didn't go over very well because for the most part we all froze when all eyes from the church were upon us expecting us to really SAANNG. Instead, all they could hear were my sisters and I sing the chorus repetitiously as if the needle on the record player was stuck; we were harmonizing but absolutely terrified of performing in front of people.

As a preteen, I became stressed, depressed and worried daily over what seemed to me, to be my never ending growth spurt. I'd come home, run upstairs to my room, drop my bags and go straight to her room and get into bed with her, and while we lay on pillows, I'd tell her all the names the kids called me for the day and cry. My mother would always say, "Danni you're pretty, they'll see; watch".

Some weeks were so tough for me and I'd tell my mother I didn't want to go to school. She would always just say, "OK," and not question me on whether or not I was sick or had over slept, etc. She knew the reason; I'd had my fill of the name calling and deserved a break.

And lastly one of my powerful memories of my mother occurred while I was in high school. My Algebra teacher had given me an F for a reason unknown to me. So I brought all my graded assignments home showing my mother that I'd actually earned an A but my teacher gave me an F. She got out of the bed that day, my assignments in tow, met with my teacher and I received an A instead of an F. I was so happy; first because she came to my school, but also because she was so pretty and people would (finally) have an opportunity to see MY beautiful mother.

Chapter 6: MY EARLIEST MEMORIES OF MY FATHER

All during my childhood, I was told that I looked just like my father. My first memory of him was when I was about 6 or 7 years old. He would come by periodically to visit, after providing my mother with his infamous--SHORT NOTICE! This made his visits even more annoying to my mother. Along with knowing her children perceived our father as the greatest thing in the world, she hated that we loved him but wanted us to love him at the same time. We also knew during these sporadic visits, our father would sometimes come bearing gifts and I knew one would always be for me. I always felt, secretly, that I was my father's favorite child.

During one of his visits, I peeked into my mother's room and overheard the whispers of an argument. I observed the hostility brewing, as my mother told him, "You have more than one child. Why didn't you bring something for all your kids, Donny?" My father would reply with a half-hearted, yet charismatic chagrin, "I will next time." Scared, my heart sank as I prayed he would be able to stay for a little while longer and that I would still be allowed to receive that boxed gift he was holding.

Thank God he answered my prayer, as I got both; he was allowed to stay for awhile and I got my gift. Our dad usually began his visits with his "Hey baby" greetings as he lifted each of us up to give us a hugs and kisses. Once he gave me the box, I tore into it immediately and found a long ivory dress. It was soooo pretty and frilly, like me. The bottom of the dress swept the floor on me. As a child, I'd seen other little girls with these types of dresses on. I felt there couldn't possibly be a long dress that could actually fit me because I was so tall, BUT my dad found one. That meant so much to me!

Our father was a handsome man with a wide bright white smile. He had long soft curls that swung gently along his jacket collar, yet some managed to dangle, ever so slightly down his back. Long, permed, straight hair was the style back then and his hair was longer than some women. He was always dressed in a suit, with hints of cologne dashed here and there, a hat with a brim- tilted to the side along with a handkerchief tucked in his suit's pocket. Our father smoked cigarettes, cigars, and/or tobacco he stuffed in a brown wood pipe. He was such a distinguished and elegant looking man. You could see the twinkling in his eye during his visits. My father felt like he was on top of the world, as he was hanging out with all of his girls.

He knew it didn't take much to entertain us. He would blow smoke rings into the air and laugh hysterically as my sisters and I argued over who would be first to wave their hands in the air to dissolve the smoke rings as they spread aimlessly into the air. When I was small, I loved the smell of cigarette smoke because it reminded me of the times we'd spent with our dad. His presence was our little exposure to "worldly things". This alone seemed to make him even more interesting to us "church going" children.

At a very young age, I was very conscientious of my height. This stemmed from the way in which people would greet me as a child. I observed the shock on their faces, as they'd realize my height in comparison to my age and this embarrassed me. My mother was a strikingly beautiful, young woman herself which was what brought our presence to people's attention. When she'd enter a room, a store, or church with her three girls, people would stop her. First to tell her how pretty ALL of her girls were and then they'd ask the God awful question, "How old are they?" Lights, camera, action, I'd instantly be placed on display. All the twisting and turning would begin as they'd begin to compare my height to that of either their child of similar age or worst, my height to their adult height. They'd then move to my hair which was another ATTENTION grabber. They would say things like, "Oh my God," they'd say, "her hair is so long and pretty." As a painfully shy little girl, in a large body, all the interest would cause my stomach to ache. I was too young to decipher that all the curiosity was not always negative, as I'd internalized and initially thought.

Although my mother always appeared to be very aggravated with my father during his sporadic visits, she still always allowed us with spend time with him in our home or to go with him when he came by. She never told me or my siblings why she was so upset with him. So off we went to spend time with our dad. I was particularly excited during the time spent with him because my height and hair didn't matter when I was with him. You see, our father had hair just like mine and he was also very tall.

On our outings, we'd either go out to eat, go to his apartment and he'd cook or he'd take us to our Grandmother's house. My father was an excellent cook. When he would cook, we'd sit down quietly and wait because his apartment was messy. That didn't matter much to us because we were spending time with him. He'd try to expose us to different things like kumquats and oysters and his wild political views. Needless to say, I couldn't stomach either food item. Kumquats tasted like a weird tangerine and just watching him slurp down the slimy, dripping flesh of a raw oyster was all I needed to see to know it wasn't going to make it to my lips, let alone into my mouth!

The times he decided to bring us to our Grandma's (his mother's) house, I'd instantly try to become invisible, hiding behind his legs until I felt comfortable. My dad always stood way back on his legs too so there was plenty of room for me to hide. Our Grandmother's house was always busy and festive, being that my father's families were very free spirited people. They would express themselves amongst each other, while all the latest R & B, Jazz, and Soul music filled the house. Some of our family lived upstairs, in the rust colored house with the beautifully manicured front lawn. Others would stop by daily after work to get a bite to eat, fellowship, dance, snap their fingers, and clap their hands, as they'd sashay to the different songs bellowing all throughout the house. This was all while continuing to eating something our Grandmother had cooked in large pots on the stove or wrapped in aluminum foil on the counter tops in the kitchen... it used to smell so good.

My father would eventually peel me off his leg and leave. He never stayed that long at his mother's house. I wasn't sure why he didn't stay and I never asked him why because I didn't mind the arrangement at all. We were spending time with our "Ma'am-ma"- that is the special name we all so affectionately called her. "Ma'am-ma's" house was not only filled with our dad's siblings, our cousins, various friends, food and lots of laughter, but we had open, unsupervised access to her jewelry, furs and knickknacks that she had stashed all throughout the house. Also at "Ma'am - ma's" house they didn't seem to make as much of a fuss about my height, which put me at ease because a lot of our father's family were also very tall and statuesque. Our father knew "Ma'am-ma" would allow us to roam freely and we had LOTS of cousins to play with all the time. We'd all play dress up and sometimes erupt into arguments over who was going to wear which fur or jewelry piece first, second and third. Ma'am-ma would intervene from time to time and give everyone a piece of something. Heck, she had more than enough to go around anyway.

Ma'am-ma was a socialite because people would drop in at various times and she always had food and activities for everyone to do. So during our visits, she would sometimes interrupt our play briefly and introduce my cousins, siblings and me to her company. I remember we were always introduced as "Donny's daughters" then gasps came as people would say, "Oh my God, she (me) looks just like him!" when they got to me. That statement alone made me feel so proud. I'd wear that compliment on my chest like a badge of honor. I looked like my dad.

Soon after this, my father's purchases would soon fade. In my whole life, I remember receiving two other gifts from my dad- an onyx heart ring with a small diamond chip in the center of the heart and, a purple amethyst ring which was my birthstone, he gave me at my high school graduation. I still have that ring. That is some of my earliest memories of our father, our dad.

Chapter 7: ANOTHER BABY GIRL

I remember when my mother was leaving to go to the hospital to have Sunni, and her asking me to lotion her legs. As I rubbed her legs with lotion she said, "I'm going to have the baby now." I was so excited, it was like I was having a baby too and no longer did we have to hear, "Lauren is the baby, let her have it; Lauren is the baby give it to her." To this day, I remember her due date, May 10th, but Sunni decided to come early. She was born on May 1st. She was so cute with her bald head, but when it grew in it was sandy brown, almost blonde. Her skin color was also golden brown; she had large pink lips and a feisty personality from day one.

Sunni primarily slept in a crib in my mother's room. Shortly after her birth, I would become responsible for watching her also. On one particular day, Sunni kept being found wandering away and of course getting me in trouble. I became determined to figure out how she kept getting out of her crib; besides Sunni was just a baby who at that time couldn't even walk. So one day I noticed after I'd put her in her crib and begin cleaning, she'd always end up crawling up next to me. So I put her back in her crib, pulled up my mother's bedroom door and watched her through the crack in the door. Once Sunni realized the door was closed, she popped up and into action. She grabbed the rails of her crib and began to climb out of the crib onto the dresser. She then crawled across the dresser, swung her little body over the ledge and then dropped herself down to the floor and began get into EVERYTHING, eventually crawling out the door and up to me. She was a very smart and determined little girl.

I remember one day my siblings and I were outside playing and we heard this scream of conviction coming from our mother. She yelled across the court, "DANNI, MEGAN AND LAUREN! WHERE IS SUNNI? You know you all were supposed to be watching her!!!" We shrugged our shoulders, motioning that we didn't know because we'd been outside playing, and that Sunni was inside with her. Acknowledging how serious this could be, we all ran up and down the hill and then back to the house because we couldn't find her. Sadly, we looked at our mother, who was on the phone calling family and friends. After she got off the phone she looked at us but just that minute something told my mother to look in the end wood coffee table with the little small compartment in the living room. There she was...Sunni had heard all the commotion but sat quietly, looking. She then began to laugh which made all of us laugh.

Sunni was a very happy baby, laughing often at people. She was cute but also very smart. We didn't mind bringing Sunni around because her intelligence was like having a puppet on your lap for show. She was tiny but could talk at an early age and made sense. I didn't mind watching Sunni. She made life interesting.

On one of our many outings Sunni got into an argument with our neighbor, Jerry. Jerry was teenager who happened to also be older than me as I was in junior high school and he was in high school. Sunni must have been about 3 or 4 years old and Jerry started picking at Sunni as we were walking past him because she didn't have any hair. My mother did everything to try to keep some hair on her head but every inch that managed to grow would

40

quickly be snatched out by Sunni, leaving her with a few strands of sandy brown, patchy, fluffy fuzz. My mother would put hats on her head when we took her out. But that was a fight because Sunni was shameless in her baldness. When Jerry noticed that Sunni had no hair, he blurted out, "Ha, ha, ha, look at her bald head!" Everyone around us laughed. But Sunni, who was shameless in her baldness, retorted back, "Ha, ha, ha datz why your breathe stinks!" And everyone roared as they fell over, grabbing their stomachs in deep belly laughter. What made this interaction EXTREMELY funny was the fact that Sunni was a baby, standing knee height to the great big high school student. Everyone could see Jerry's feelings were really hurt. I think that was the day I fell in love with Sunni.

For some reason, this period of my life is foggy. I don't remember when Naveh was born. I don't remember if we were living up the hill or down the hill. All that I do remember during that time was that I was always on edge with trying to deal with all of my responsibilities as the oldest sibling and deal with the extreme pressure of becoming an athlete, when I was so girly.

I continued to want more freedom. However, my mother would seldom allow that, so of course my siblings and I began to sneak out and do things like going to see boyfriends and/or go to a party without permission. My mother would eventually birth my brother, A.D., from her new husband, Mr. Abdul, just as I left to attend college in upstate Connecticut.

Chapter 8: HE DIDN'T TAKE HIS LITHIUM

"Your father is mentally ill" is a verdict I grew comfortable with hearing repeatedly from adults; however, it provided my parents with an excuse to continue to drag their children through a life filled with traumatic events and unrelenting instability within our home. "Danni, you know your dad is manic depressant; it's now called Bipolar; he just will not take his lithium," was an excuse that was used daily as my father was allowed to come in and out of our young lives.

Furthermore, we were advised that we should be able to tell when he's not taking his meds by the changes in his weight. These warnings would almost become a song, sang by my mother daily, when she spoke about my father and his illness. This information was partially explanatory for my mother as she justified my fathers' strange behaviors and her inability to protect us because he was our father; thus had rights to us.

"Oh Lord, Donny didn't take his Lithium again," were the words we heard just before my father would begin acting strange and then disappear. As a child, I often wondered why he didn't just take his Lithium. My father would continue to come to our apartment both unannounced and announced on any random occasion all though out our childhood. As we got older with exposure and interaction with "normal people," his behaviors grew increasingly more weird, scary and eventually embarrassing.

During one of his sporadic visits, we were told our father had shaved all the hair off his body. My mother, in her quest to find a way to handle this situation, was in a major tizzy. She was horrified as she looked at him and began to process in her head, and out loud, how she would prepare her children to see their dad, while trying to scold him for even coming to the house and presenting himself this way.

What our mother failed to realize is she had been very successful in teaching us how to love him unconditionally, so at that time in our lives it didn't matter what he looked like. We adored our father so much it never mattered when he came or what state of mind he was in at the time of his visits. So whenever we heard our father downstairs we were immediately excited. He'd been MIA for a while so we would finally be able to spend time with him and we didn't care how he looked.

During this particular "drop by," we stood together at the top of the steps jumping up and down, excited and anxiously awaiting clearance from our mother to begin our visit with our father. Although my mother was ambivalent to our excitement she always gave in and allowed his visits, but this time she provided us with forewarning-- asking us not to stare. She said, "Listen, your dad decided to cut all his hair off his body. Don't be scared." We jumped down the stairs two steps at a time, almost knocking each other over as we're each trying to be the first to jump into his arms. As I got down the stairs, I looked directly at my father's face. First, noticing his big bright smile was still there but then I noticed he didn't have any eyebrow or eyelashes. He did look weird. So, I asked him why did he cut his hair off. He told me because it (his hair) was not clean. His hairless appearance didn't matter to us; we were just overjoyed being in his presence. Shortly after this visit, he would later have a mental breakdown and be placed back in a mental institution.

Chapter 9: MY FIRST SEPARATION

I remember the whispers days before the eventual decision for us to have to leave our apartment came to fruition. My mother came to me one day after school, and said, "Danni we have to leave our apartment for a while because your dad hasn't been taking his Lithium". So I need you to go quickly and pack some clothing for yourself, and then come help pack some clothes for your sisters." My father had completed his stay in the mental institution, however, quickly began to decompensate again. She went on further to tell me the sleeping arrangements and this is what crushed me. I was told I would be staying with Sister Jones but that she and my three sisters: Megan, Sunni and Lauren would be staying with Sister Matthews. I was very upset but obedient, as I quickly packed, all the while thinking to myself, "Why do I have to stay with Sister Jones?" I wanted to be with my family but I didn't complain; whatever the reason was for this decision, it seemed urgent and I didn't want to stress my mother out.

Both Sisters Matthews' and Jones' apartments were literally right across the street from our apartment in the housing project. So I was able to calm myself some by thinking, "I'm not going to be very far from my family; this plan is temporary so I am willing to go along with the plan." Then I also thought this plan was very strange because our father didn't even live with us so why did we have to leave? Why couldn't he just stop coming over for a while like usual?

At that point in my life I'd never slept outside our apartment other than a sleep over and I still always wanted to go home. I'd even spent long hot summers in Charlotte, NC with my maternal grandmother in the South which my mother and all my family knew I HATED. Despite our rough relationship, I just hated being away from my mother, my sisters and my home.

After we were all packed, we all travelled across the street. I went to Sister Jones' house and the rest of my family went to Sister Matthews' house. I felt puzzled as I thought about the fact that we were not far enough to say we were truly hiding from my father; so why did we have to leave?

Even as school began we didn't change our daily routine. We continued to attend Stamford Elementary School and daily church services. However, with all the abrupt changes I was upset and depressed, because I still struggled to understand why mother told us that this move was because of my father. I still wasn't sure if he was really looking for us. Had he been menacing towards my mother (that wasn't anything out of the normal)? Why would this trigger her decision to uproot her entire family even if it was temporary? My mother had done such a good job in making sure we didn't hate our father yet she failed to share her struggles, hurts and disappointment with him. To add to our confusion she'd stayed with him so the confusion with this move remained unanswered. So we in turn would always love him unconditionally as we did not recognize or realize at our young ages that he actually inadvertently would cause us to suffer a great deal of emotional pain for many years.

Living with Sister Jones was different; she had a good job at IBM. She dressed really nice as she left for work daily. Her house was spotless and completely furnished with quality furniture. Sister Jones' home was like a museum; it was in a constant state of organization and cleanliness; her refrigerator was even clean. The atmosphere of her home almost seemed sterile and museum like, so I was very careful not to touch or break anything.

Sister Jones was a true "diva divorcee" with two well cared for little girls. Tonya was the oldest and she also happened to be my best childhood friend and her little sister Tina was just a few years younger than us. Sister Jones had me sleep in Tina's bed. Tonya slept in her bed and Tina slept with their mother. Their bedroom had two beautiful matching white beds, with matching white and pink sheet and comforter sets.

Mr. Jones , Ms. Jones' ex-husband, not only paid his child support on time, but he visited often, brought his girl's clothing, lots of gifts and even spent quality time with them. Thus, Tonya and Tina always had their hair done neatly, they were always dressed in clean, fashionable clothing, had the latest toy/gadget and their refrigerator and food closet was always stocked to capacity. Looking in from the outside, it always appeared as if the Jones' family had it all, which made me feel depressed and want to go home all the more.

At home we didn't have all the material items that the Jones' had but that didn't matter to me. At my home I had my own family, my own bed, in my own room that I shared with my own sisters. So all I dreamed about at night was going home or of hearing a date when I would be going home. I mean, don't get me wrong, the Jones' family was very nice to me, but it didn't stop my silent pain and deep desire to be with MY family. Furthermore, my mother never followed up to share with me why any of this was happening and when it all was going to end. All I noted during this time was there were a lot more grown up whisper sessions. So I continued to go to school daily, come home with Tonya and Tina and watch them engage in their daily cleaning routines.

My feeling of depression grew deeper as I felt more lonely and isolated, longing to be with my family. I was also not allowed to go visit my mother and my sisters as often as I wanted to because, as my mother explained, she was staying with someone and she didn't want to have too much traffic coming in and out of Sister Matthews' apartment. Periodically this arrangement got to be too much for me and I'd cry; if someone saw my tears (even though I'd often hide and cry) my mother would be called. She would send for me to come over Sister Mathews' house. My mother would give me a hug; wipe my tears but she still she wasn't able to tell me when we'd be going home. So even with the sporadic tear filled breakdowns, I'd still have to return to Sister Jones' home. As the days turned into weeks and the weeks turned into months, I began to feel like I was continuously dragging my bag of depressed, sadness and isolation along with me daily.

My mother would eventually receive urgent word via our neighbors that she needed to check on her apartment because they noticed that her husband had been acting strange. He had been seen throwing LARGE amounts of clothing and other items into the dumpster at the beginning of our apartment complex. Again, I didn't hear very much about what was transpiring because the adult whisper sessions had been moved behind closed doors, versus in the other room. My mother sent for me when I arrived at Sister Mathews' apartment. I noticed her eyes were intensely red and seemed to be brimming with tears. This time she would share with me, Megan and Lauren that something had happened at our house and we would be staying where we were at for a little while longer. I didn't know how to respond to this news. I felt crushed under the intense weight of my depression but I could not show our mother because she looked distraught and I didn't want to burden her with my feelings.

She went on further to explain that our father had been taken back to Old Town Mental Institution and that he was out of our apartment, but he destroyed it so we couldn't go home right away. We would have to stay a little longer while our Uncles came to fix our apartment. She further explained that my father had thrown some of our clothes out into the big dumpster. I vaguely remember people going into the dumpster to retrieve what they could and that bothered me, but I managed to survive by hoping we would be home soon. For the next few weeks my Uncles, Mike and Roy, would come by daily to help my mother prepare our apartment for our return.

My mother was too depressed during this time to continue to check on me to make sure I was ok. So, I dealt with the shame of the act my father committed and lack of privacy through this tough time, alone. Even though this was a tough time, I didn't take any days off from school .One day, one of my friends from school (who didn't live in our neighborhood) asked me if my father was crazy, I took a deep breath as a way to suck up the tears, looked at the person and didn't answer. I was completely devastated. However, I'd mastered the art of internalizing my pain as a way to make it through school daily. I had thought to myself the only person that knew what was going on with my family was my best friend, Tonya. For some strange reason it never dawned on me that all the neighbors in our community knew what happened

49

because of the amount of people who were involved in repairing all the damage. I rushed home from school that day and told my mother, who was preoccupied with grief, hurt and sadness, over what happened. She didn't display very much concern nor did she respond thoughtfully. She just said, "Don't worry about it". No reassurance, no encouragement, just, "don't worry about it;" and to be honest, I tried really hard to do just that- "don't worry about it".

After about a month of being kept from our apartment, I finally received word that we would be returning to our home. I was so happy; I remember my mother meeting with us in an attempt to prepare me and my siblings for the sight of any damage that was not able to be repaired; like the gashes in her furniture, random paint splatter, etc., but Uncle Mike and Roy fixed all that they could and so now we could go home soon. That was a very happy day for me.

Chapter 10: WE FOUND THE PICTURES

After our return home, we were engaged in our regular weekend housecleaning sprees, when one of my sisters stumbled upon some pictures; she summoned me to come and look at them. So Megan, Lauren and I stepped away from our chores to look at them. Looking at the photos, we're finally able to piece together the limited information we'd been told about what happened to our apartment. As we looked at all the pictures our mouths dropped open at the extent of all the destruction. One picture stood out to us the most, and that was of our mother. In this picture she appeared to be cowering over while receiving assistance walking. People were on both side of her holding her up, assisting her to walk; she was crying. A few saints, (people from our church), who were also our neighbors, were her helping walk through all the debris in our apartment. Inside our home, Uncle Roy and Mike were there; they were both surveying and documenting all the damage.

We continued to look at the pictures and observing not just my mother's personal belongings, but all of our precious belongings savagely being thrown to the floor. There were piles and piles of clothing, food, pictures, etc., covering all the floors in the entire apartment. Everyone in the pictures were standing ankle deep in all the stuff on the floor. Paint and canned food items had been opened and slung upon intermittent walls, furniture had gashes while all the doors of my mother's dressers were hanging by the screws. It looked like a bomb had been set off in our home.

We were now able to understand what had happened to our home. I thought to myself, "my mother must have been scared of our father and felt he was going to hurt her; so that's why we left." I guess her plan was to leave him in the house because he was acting really weird with HOPES that he'd eventually leave on his own. Instead our father stayed in our apartment. He was not really looking for us because we were right across the street, but I guess he just grew angrier as he realized we weren't coming home.

He had destroyed every room in our apartment. I mean, literally- the kitchen, living room, bathroom, stairway and both bedrooms. He'd thrown everything he could find on shelves and in drawers, on the floor. He then began throwing our clothing in the big dumpster outside at the beginning of our court (row of apartments); which is what must have alerted the neighbors.

I thank God for our caring neighbors. They'd been hearing the ruckus for a few nights but were uncertain about how to approach our father because they'd known him to be overall strange, but never violent. So our neighbors, knowing that we'd gone to stay across the street at Sister Jones' and Sister Mathews', thought it necessary to contact our mother when our father started throwing large amounts of clothing and other large items into the dumpster.

I have this last additional memory and I'm not sure if it's true- about this tragic event. I'd already noted that my Barbie doll house still stood untouched amidst all the debris, however, I also vaguely remember my mother telling me with discord, that my father hadn't cut my mattress. This stuck with me in particular because of the piercing hurt I'd felt as my mother seemed senselessly mad at me; while at the same time I also felt special because my father showed me love, even in his craziness. Remember, I'm not sure if this is true; it could have been a way in which God protected my precious, innocent heart and mind in the midst of this tragedy.

The relationship I have with my father remains emotionless, but I love him and I do know he loves me. Sometimes I wonder where my emotions lay when it comes to the concerns about my father, but just as long as I know he's alive, I'm good. I love him but I don't know what aspect of my life to trust him with, as he has always been mentally unstable.

Chapter 11: LIFE WOULD EVENTUALLY TURN TO (OUR) NORMAL

After this incident, my mother began to sleep more. As one could imagine, she began putting more and more responsibilities upon me as "the oldest". Cooking, cleaning, and assigning the rotational chores and non-physical forms of disciplining my younger siblings. As my mother forbade physical discipline amongst her children, I had to be creative in finding ways to get my siblings to follow my directions. This was more of an issue for me because I knew if things weren't taken care of, it would be my fault. So in turn, I became driven and passionate about finding ways for things to be completed around the house and completed correctly. It was like hearing the words "IT'S YOUR FAULT!" haunting me all throughout my childhood and teenage life; and believe it or not even now as an adult hearing those words causes me to experience some anxiety and stress.

I became manic and anal retentive in EVERY area of my life as I began to run within myself anything to get away from the words, "IT'S YOUR FAULT". This also began to manifest into my obsession with how I would keep things in and about my life clean and organized at all times. All clothing in my drawers was always laid neatly and organized in some fashion. All my personal items-deodorant, lotions, powders, perfumes, lip gloss, which sat atop of my drawer were stood up and arranged neatly. My bed was always made up immediately after I got up and remained in a constant state of tidiness and order; if I or someone sat on my bed I'd immediately fix and pull the sheets tight again when they got up. My clothing was always hung up neatly. My need for a constant state of organization was so intense that I'd place every one of my personal items with such precision that I could tell if anyone touched my stuff and I'd immediately be on the attack. I even went so far as to write notes and place them on my personal things, i.e. combs, brushes- in order to give my siblings a heads up that I'd know if they'd scrounged through my drawers.

I still can't stand the SIGHT of dirty, dust, and/or disorder because seeing it hurts me emotionally and somehow physically; I feel stressed, panicky and sweaty. So, if I come upon something that appears dirty or unorganized, I'll immediately clean or straighten it out. Quite naturally this madness within my mind caused even more emotional distancing and strife between my siblings and I. Although my siblings are ALL very clean also, they did not share the emotional chaos, to my knowledge, that I felt behind my obsession with cleanliness.

Although, I never really physically fought my sisters, our periodic arguments may have resulted in some pushing, grabbing and yelling at each other, nose to nose, but that's about it. As one could imagine, they didn't always listen to me but that didn't matter, we still had to get the chores done. If it got too hectic around the house and no one was listening, the final straw would be played out in a way that caused everyone too stress in our house...we'd mess up each other's beds. Piece by piece we'd mess each other's beds up; first ripping   pillows off the bed and throwing them to the floor. Then the next sibling, who was involved in this particular quarrel, may pull the sheets and then the blanket's off of that sister's bed, etc. This would go on until all beds were complete undressed, having no blanket's, pillows or sheets. Then we'd stress as we quickly remade our beds before our mother noticed the mess; so even our fights involved the need for cleanliness and constant order.

The end result of my failure to get my siblings to listen was me being placed on punishment. So for the most part of my childhood, I stayed on punishment. Our mother often yelled the word "PUNISHMENT" which crushed our world, but this was her way of maintaining control over us. Her "punishment" entailed a combination of either getting hit with a belt, a comb or on rare occasions, a switch, no TV, no phone or no outside and/or one of the aforementioned. One thing I appreciated about our mother during these times is that she did not physically discipline us often. More than likely because it would require her to move physically and she preferred to allow days to past stagnantly, sitting quietly in her room, lying in bed. We'd often hear her yell from her bed "PUNISHMENT" which would cause our life to stop, as it barred us from going outside for up to a week or two; sometimes even a month; so when this statement was a threat; we definitely froze in the midst of our trouble.

No outside punishment meant staying in your bedroom, not being able to attend any scheduled after school activities such as the after school program at the Boys and Girls Club, when I was in elementary school and junior high school. But in high school this meant no basketball practice.

I spent most of my adolescence days and nights lying across my bed reading. My love for reading grew out of what seemed constant placement on punishment. Reading took me many places; it allowed me to go to different cities, countries and worlds. It made me laugh, and it made me cry. It provided answers to my questions about what to expect as I grew older, etc. Reading was my outlet to all of the craziness occurring in my world. So the threat about being on punishment didn't bother me as much because I knew I could always read and leave my room anyway.

After destroying our home, our father remained in Old Town, a mental health facility, for a few months and we began visiting him from time to time. As a child, I often felt anxious and scared to visit because my thoughts swirled; wondering would he ever answer why he'd destroyed our home. Was he angry? When he was cutting, ripping, tearing and throwing away our things, would he have stopped if he saw me? All would play itself out continuously in my mind when we were visiting our father at the mental institution. While at the same time, I always felt happy because he was my Dad and I was going to see him (again) so, I was willing to work through the uneasy feelings.

On one particular day our paternal grandmother had contacted my mother and arranged for us to all go up and have lunch with our father. Excited yet petrified, I was able to focus my attention on the fact that I was about to have an opportunity to see my father and spend time with him. However, my mind would race between joyful thoughts and paralyzing fears of again seeing all the zombie like people walk the grounds and halls aimlessly, BUT we would be able to see our father. Equally important was we'd been told that he would be getting out soon, so I was even more willing to go. When my grandmother arrived, I took a look at all the foods she's packed for our visit…it all looked so yummy. She'd made chicken, her famous cabbage with sausage, potato salad and cake. Despite my fears and excitement, we headed to the facility to visit our father.

Old Town was a large, white facility surround by a beautiful, well manicured, woodsy garden. Once we parked we proceeded to walk towards the large building with the big glass doors. Once inside we walked down a large hallway with lots of doors and into the visitation area. This room seemed to serve as a lounge area too. I observed several people, some of which who were visiting with their loved ones; while others (patients), were either staring at us or aimlessly at the ceiling, walls or out the window.

Our hearts were beating fast as we immediately walked up to the receptionist desk with my grandmother and mother as they gave our names and identification so that we could begin our visit. Finally, they went to get my father. He was cleanly shaven with street clothes on. He always came out appearing aggravated at his peers, waiting for anyone of them to say something he felt was out of the way so he could go off. My father was indignant and arrogant as he proclaimed his normality and their CRAZINESS; which was his usual song and dance. You see, our father always felt he'd been placed in this institution mistakenly.

I sat constantly on guard during these visits watching and visualizing, in my head a way out, as I watched people while maintaining an arm's length distance from my grandmother or my mother. I figured they were the only ones who could help me if one of those people tried to get me.

During one of our visits this man stood up and calmly, walked over to the water fountain, he bent over and as the water began to sprout up he made a loud crackly, wet cough and brought up a large amount of phlegm, spewing the matter at the water fountain. The man then stood there and watched his bodily fluids splatter and slide down the head of the water fountain. Let's just say to this very day, will I not drink at water fountains public and/or private.

Just at that moment, my father yelled at the man as he'd noticed what the man was doing. I couldn't eat any of the food my grandmother had made for us as I began to have repeated flashbacks of that mucus dripping down the water fountain. As I watched that man and my father I realized that most mentally ill individuals feel that they are not crazy. My father was in a stable place mentally at that moment but he was very angry about even being placed in a mental institution because he felt he wasn't crazy, like them.

Chapter 12: THE UNEMPLOYED, SINGLE MARRIED WOMEN

I can only remember my mother working two jobs during my childhood. One was at Dictaphone and the other was at Saysha, which were two small private corporations. During these times that she'd worked she would always come home complaining. She would always end up in tears, describing some form of ill-treatment she'd suffered at the hands of some insensitive co-worker. The victim role is what my mother embraced most as an employee, which ultimately always led to a reason for her to either quit or was at the root of her eventual termination. My mother never was the type of person to do a self evaluation in order to determine what she may be doing to contribute to her repeated failures in the workforce.

Therefore, my 5 siblings and I grew up without a role model or stories of how to be a successful employee. We survived mostly on welfare benefits, or income maintenance as they called it during those time, and whatever handouts family and friends provided when my mother's complaining or sadness became unbearable for them to continue to hear.

I'm not sure if my mother ever filed for child support but, I do know she'd ask our Dad for help from time to time, but she knew that was a battle already lost as my father would purposely have a nervous breakdown, according to our Mother, in order to not have to pay child support.

Chapter 13: FEELING LIKE A CIRCUS ACT

My middle school years were filled with memories of my SERIOUS growth spurt along with constant reminders of just how poor we really were. As I grew in height, I was unable to fit into my mother's clothing, and shoes. I remember having my weight and height checked in 7th grade; I was 5'll, at 12 years old. I was always weighed down with great anxiety, as I was constantly thinking to myself, "am I ever going to stop growing?" I would have nightmares about possibly being a performer for the circus because I was convinced either way that I was a "freak of nature." To make matters worse, my skin broke out unmercifully. Unsure of how to handle it my mother (trying to motivate me to wash my face more often) would say things like, "Danni you have bumps on top of bumps!" Not to mention she couldn't afford to purchase skincare products like other mothers so I did the best I could. Instead, I never felt motivated to listen to her since; because I did wash my face several times a day and it still broke out.

Day after day, I went to school and endured entire days of name calling. I remember being called names such as "Lurch", "Too Tall Jones "or "Big Foot" when I'd pass in the halls, as many peers laughed. I felt so ugly. So, as a way to stop the name calling, I fought a lot during middle school. I was suspended and/or placed in school detention so many times that the Principal's words to me after what would be my last fight was, "Danielle, would you like to go to school with people like yourself, people who fight all the time, because that's my recommendation; for your high school placement." His words changed my mindset about fighting; I was bad, but not bad enough to want to be in a school where I would never stop fighting.

Being tall was very hard for me. I had maybe three outfits for the week. Tall clothing in regular stores didn't fit me. One time my mother purchased me two pair of pants- one was bright orange and the other was bright yellow. I came up with an idea of how I was going to make these pants fit me well because they were both too short. So, I cut off the bottom of both pants and sewed the extra material on the pants which then gave me two long pair of pants. One day I'd have on the orange ones with yellow bottoms and the next day I'd have on the yellow ones with the orange bottoms.

My hair was always fine and about shoulder length so the only style I could master on my own was a ponytail. I wanted so badly to get baby edges. I remember one day I came up with a way to get them so I parted my hair about an inch in from my face and cut it all the way around. Once it was cut, I applied grease and water to the shortened hair and attempted to brush it down for baby edges but instead of it lying down like my friends did, it curled up around my face and I looked like a lion.

My mother didn't take very much interest in the fact that I was growing up and I had teenager needs, feelings and concerns. She slept most of that time in my life away. I remember her room was always dark; her being in her bra and nightgown under the covers telling me to prepare dinner and make sure the house was clean. I stayed on punishment because I couldn't consistently get my sisters to listen to me and do their chores. There were also times during one of my mother's inspections of dishes I'd washed that she found a speck of dirt, so she pushed the entire rack of dishes back in the sink to be rewashed and then she grounded me to my room for weeks.

As you know, I really didn't mind being punished because I was a bookworm. I read and left the city, the country the world in books. I loved stories about people. I read about things that concerned me, like my budding sexuality; my mother didn't explain that to me so, I found a book that did. The only thing that I was always allowed as a teenager, even if I were on punishment, was to go to church.

I was a member of the choir and the youth group. At church no one really picked on me and I fit in somewhat but I was still a McKnight girl, so I always felt people were talking about me and that they thought less of me and my siblings. This was partly because my mother in her quest for assistance always made our lives, our problems, our struggles, public to the church. Yet, I never knew what was going on in their homes but everyone from the child to the parent knew what was going on in mine.

Chapter 14: YOUTH FELLOWSHIP

Due to my church, I got to hang with some cool girls and a few boys and my mother didn't mind because I was at church and she knew their parents were saved. So, that equated to her having no issues. I loved my church friends so much. They were normal in spite of all the hype about going to church and being Christians. Some even had boyfriends and were allowed to hang out with them.

When I was with my friends from church I could hang out. We'd go to the movies, go over their homes or just drive all over town because one of my friends had a car. They shared their struggles with me and supported me through mine. The church organized a lot of activities for us in the church too. We had parties and socials and I watched them develop plays and more.

I was still painfully shy and was never forced to do much more than sing in the choir. I did it only because I enjoyed it. At times during my visits to some of my friend's homes, I noted their parents were a little protective of them, as if they thought I would somehow be a bad influence on their kid; honestly, I think it was because I lived in the projects, but I wasn't doing anything more than their children were doing.

Chapter 15: SO I BECAME A WOMAN

I got my period at 13 while I was down south in Gastonia, North Carolina for the summer. I didn't know what it was instead; I thought I was bleeding to death. I kept changing my panties, but the blood kept coming. So I called my cousin, who was really one of my grandmother's foster children, and asked her to come into the bathroom so I could show her but, when she did, she didn't know what it was either. So, we finally decided to wait until my Aunt Sonia came home and told her that something was wrong with me.

When my cousin told Sonia, I sat quietly in the other room waiting to see what she was going to say and/or do to help me but, she immediately got on the phone and called my mother saying, "Danni's a woman." I still didn't get it; I had no idea what she was talking about. So she took me in the car and we went to the store. Although it was a warm, sunny day outside, it seemed as if we'd driven through the beginning and end of a rain storm. It was pouring in the front of the car but outside it was bright and sunny. When we were in the car she explained to me that the bleeding was my menstrual cycle and then purchased my first pack of pads.

Even though I was a woman, I didn't feel like a woman. I was still very tall and VERY skinny. I loved girly things- dresses, and high heels, but my mother never could afford to buy me any. I also couldn't wear "hand me downs" because 9 times out of 10 my foot was bigger than the adult who would give their shoes to us.

High school was when I first got approached by the girl's basketball coach. I come from a family of 5 girls. I tried out, but at that point in my life I didn't even know how many points you got when you shot and made a basket, let alone which basket to shoot in; that had me nervous for years. I struggled with finding interest in being sweaty and wearing sneakers daily. The running was CRAZY to me; the preseason conditioning was also CRAZY to me. I stuck with it because my cousin Rebbie felt it was a good thing and she would always talk to me about it. She worked in Stamford High School, so she'd come to my class if she were told I was not trying, thinking about giving up or had quit; which I would do at least once all four years of high school.

Basketball made me mentally tougher. I used to fight people on the street but now I could fight on the court, but I had to learn to take the tenacity and fight for rebounds and make myself big when posting up. During that time I had lived through so much pain in my life that I couldn't consistently get completely into the game. But, I had a gift.

Chapter 16: WHEN I6 YEARS OLD

It was a warm October day and "Sly" came to my classroom door window signaling for me to meet him in the usual spot; in the auditorium stairwell. I was upset because we had been meeting there for a few months kissing and feeling on each other yet in the back of my head I always knew he would never make ME his girlfriend. So, this time I was going to tell him I didn't want to continue to meet anymore but he kissed me on my neck and it felt good.

I lost my focus for a moment as I began to think about not having ANYONE to fool around with. Even though our rendezvous was a secret, the extreme loneliness I experienced in my life made me long to have a boyfriend. At the same time, I knew I just couldn't allow myself to live a lie. I again tried to tell him that I didn't want to do this anymore. He tried to make me put my hands in his pants but I didn't feel comfortable, so I kept pulling back. He kept kissing me and grabbing me as I kept trying to pull away. He stopped briefly allowing me to tell him to stop again. I didn't want to do this anymore but as quickly as he stopped he again pulled me back to him; kissing me, grabbing me, holding me.

I grew aggravated and he became more aggressive. We eventually fell to the floor. He kept kissing me while holding and grabbing me around my waist, arms and my clothing. I thought to myself, "should I scream," but as quickly as that thought came, I thought I wasn't supposed be there in the first place. Before I knew it he'd pulled out his penis, began to push my panties aside as he tried to position my body so that he could penetrate me. I kept telling him "No, don't do it", but he wouldn't and didn't stop. He finally put his penis inside me as I continued to try to get away, moving myself from side to side but he was on top of me and stronger than me. I tried to grab and squeeze his penis but he'd move….it hurt, it was my first time, he never took that into consideration as he whispered in my ear angrily, "IF you don't stop I'll cum (ejaculate) inside of you." I immediately stopped, froze stiffly…and endured the pain.

I was terrified. He finally finished, wiped his self off, got up and left me there. I went straight to the girl's bathroom and felt inside my panties as it was wet; there was blood. I didn't cry; I was so scared, I tried to call my mother but she didn't answer the phone, which was unusual, as she didn't work. I walked the halls at school in a daze eventually running into my friend from church and I told her what had happened. I waited to see her response because in the back of my head I was unsure if it could have been my fault or partially my fault. However, she didn't seem to be upset by what I'd told her, so I again thought to myself, "it was my fault, no one is going to believe me."

My thoughts, "You shouldn't have been there; no one is going to believe you," flooded my mind. Along with, "he's a basketball star- tall and handsome- all the girls seemed to want him." I was a poor, ugly, bumpy faced, crooked teeth, skinny, awkwardly tall girl from the projects. Why would he do that to me, when he could have any girl in the school? He was furthermore in the "in crowd," while I was a nobody.

I would go on and tell a few more of my friends (mostly from the church) what had happened and we decided I should go to the local Planned Parenthood for an abortion if necessary; I wasn't sure if I'd even gotten pregnant. The guys from my church made me feel like they'd take care of him- not to worry, but they never did.

I eventually went home; I went straight to the bathroom, removed all my clothing, dropped my panties in the garbage and showered. Hoping I could wash all the dirt off of my body, I scrubbed and scrubbed, crying off and on. I must have stayed in there for over 2 hours. When I was finished I went straight to bed, terrorized. Thoughts of, "was it my fault?" and "if I was pregnant?" haunted me nightly for months.

Sly saw me a few days later as I was crossing the street in downtown Stamford and he came over to me and asked, "Hey are you alright?" Startled and shock at the tactlessness of the question, I looked passed him as that was all I could do at that moment. I crossed the street and that was the last time I saw him-- when I was 16 years old. I'd eventually find out it wasn't my fault after all a few years later while in college. A teacher lectured on the rape cycle; I ran out the class as my mind flooded with the memories of what had happened to me. I thought about the people I'd told and the fact that no one cared enough for me to report the crime. Thank God I am healed and made into a new creature in the name of Jesus.

Chapter 17: FORGIVES US FOR OUR TRANSGRESSIONS

The summer after completing my first year of college I was finally able to go home to spend time with my sisters. I ran up the stairs straight to my room, exhaling as I was home to spend time with my family! The transition to college had been a bit tough for me as I always hated being away from my family, my mother, and my sisters.

My mother called me to her room just as I'd laid across my bed. So, I got up and went to her room and laid across hers. I didn't give her eye contact at first, so I hadn't noticed that she was somewhat serious. I rolled over and noticed her facial expression and was unsure of what she was about to say. As a child I was always used to her telling me about the various crisis that may occur or were occurring, so I didn't think much about what she was about to say.

However what she said this time surprised me. She said, "Danni I'm pregnant." I sat straight up, giving her my full attention as I replied, "Ma, what are you going to do?" A million thoughts began to race through my mind like, "OH MY GOD! She's the Devotional Leader at church! What does this mean for her at church? What are the people at church going to think? Oh Lord! My mother sinned, she can't have this baby! OH MY GOD! My mother is going to have to have an abortion BUT that's a sin too! How does she want me to help her?"

Feeling intensely frantic and STRESSED as I looked at my mother, she looked away appearing sad. "How are you going to have the baby you're not married Ma?" I asked. She replied, "I don't know but I can't do that". I then began to panic as my mind became engulfed with thoughts of the great humiliation that our family was about to experience AGAIN.

My mother sat there in a stupor. Noticing her demeanor I found a way to calm myself down and I gave her a hug. I told my mother, "it will be fine, we'll get through this." I don't even remember talking to her about who the father was, because at this point the ONLY thing that mattered to me was that my mother was pregnant out of wedlock and that she was the devotional leader in the church and I needed to find a way to protect her.

Devastated, I had an inclination that the father of this baby was Mr. Abdul. During the last few months of my senior year in high school, my mother had begun bowling with family and friends and I got word that Mr. Abdul appeared to have been taking a liking to my mother. Mr. Abdul was a die-hard Muslim security guard at my high school. His job duties required him to catch students, who were skipping school, step in to help teachers when students became disruptive in class and other security related duties. Mr. Abdul wasn't well liked amongst many students, primarily the "bad kids," because his approach to disciplining students always bordered on excessive and inappropriate. He made it his business to not only catch kids who were choosing to skip school in various hiding places around the school campus, but he was also known to drive, chase and pick up students who were at McDonald's, Dunkin Donuts and other places that they weren't supposed to be during school hours. Once he had "captured" the students, he'd request that the "book be thrown at them". Although, I wasn't "a bad kid" and never had any personal dealings with Mr. Abdul, many of my friends were "bad kids" thus they didn't like him. So the thought of my mother now being pregnant by him was very upsetting to me.

I must admit I wasn't completely mad at my mother because I knew she must have been lonely. She'd been a single, married woman for 14 years. As a young woman myself, I don't know how she managed. My mother and I had recently gone to the court house and finalized her divorce from my father. I remember a few months prior, sitting with her in the court house until they called her name. I would eventually leave and return back to college and not know what my mother's final decision was regarding her pregnancy but I was worried. Not about the baby, but more so about how people in the church and in our family would now treat my mother.

Chapter 18: THE APOLOGY

My mother decided that she was going to go forward and carry her baby that she conceived outside of wedlock. On a Tuesday night during bible class, my mother told me she was going to address the church that evening. I agreed, but I didn't know what she was going to tell them. She didn't offer an explanation so I didn't ask; besides we were already stressed due to her pregnancy and her now visibly growing belly.

Service began as usual, but I noticed the change immediately because my mother didn't get the microphone to lead devotion. I sat back in my seat- a little sad- and watched the service go on as usual. It was understood when you "sin", I guess visually and/or chose to admit you "sinned", you step down from any position of leadership you hold in church.

Service was finally over and everyone, including children remained seated. The leaders of the church called my mother up to the front of the church. She was given the microphone and she began to shake as she said, "I'm pregnant and I'm sorry." She then began to cry. That's all I remember because once I saw her tears begin to fall my heart started beating out of my chest as feelings of anger rose to almost rage. I ran out of the church, my thoughts racing as I thought about fighting anyone and everyone. I had not been able to protect MY MOTHER! I have always had her back, especially when she was in distress. Then I began to think, "why was she was apologizing to those people?" To add further insult to my aching heart, I was aware of some of the congregants "sins" as well as those of THEIR CHILDREN. So, why was mother singled out? I HATED EVERYONE yet I still loved them, as they were all I'd known. I'd been a part of this ministry since I was 5 years old.

Brother John, our minister, came out after me attempting to console me. I'd felt like he cared but I was still very confused. I accepted the comfort from him but my tears were endless and came from a very deep place of hurt because I couldn't stop my mother's pain.

From that day on my mother, and my siblings and I were shunned in our church home. Everyone, including ministers, congregants and even their children, my childhood friends, stopped greetings us, avoided eye contact or kept conversations generic and/or short. On a sadder note, I was privy of others transgressions because a large number of the congregants and their children were my blood relatives.

Chapter 19: SHE DIDN'T TELL ME

I was now a sophomore in college; home on Winter break. I walked in the house and Megan and Lauren ran up to me excited and hugging me yelling, "DANNI!" as they did every time I came home from school. However, this time they began staring into my eyes, smiling, as they whispered amongst themselves. Lauren opened her mouth as if she wanted to tell me something but then Megan told her not to, so she stopped. My siblings always told me when things were happening in the house despite me being gone away to college. I asked Lauren to tell me because I sensed the anxiety but noticed the restraint on their faces.

I soon became aggravated because I was tired. The looks on their faces began to look silly to me. They were still staring at me, as Lauren began to physically hold her mouth as an additional measure to ensure she didn't leak the news to ME. So I gave up, moved them out of my way and began to walk upstairs to my room and unpack my clothes. Megan and Lauren followed closely behind me continuing to whisper to each other, almost tripping over themselves in an effort to keep close to me.

I noticed a change in the atmosphere of our home. The kitchen was spotlessly clean as usual but the living room was dark as I began to walk through the kitchen and upstairs towards my room. As I got to the top of the stairs, I peeked into my mother's bedroom and noticed MEN'S shoes. That was very strange.

So, I turned around to my sisters asking them who they belonged to and Lauren blurted out, "Mommy got married!" Megan pushed her, telling her, "Mommy told you not to tell her!" My heart began to race; I dropped my bags and sat on my bed as I thought about what they had just said to me. My mother got married and she didn't tell me. I knew she was pregnant by Mr. Abdul during my summer break and that was a shocker but she never told me she had plans to marry him; I just didn't like him.

My sisters walked away just as my mother and Mr. Abdul came in. My mother walked quickly up the stairs and said, "Hi!" girlishly excited. I said, "Hi," but nothing more.

Chapter 20: I'M (((NEVER))) GOING BACK

After my mother put me out of her house, I slowly walked with Tony to his house still clutching my pillow. Ms. Patricia allowed me to stay at her apartment. I slept on her couch. When I awoke we talked more about what happened and I think she thought I would consider returning home as she told me, "Your mother called". I didn't want to pressure her or make her choose sides, so I eventually walked across the street and stayed with my cousin Rebbie and her family. She'd also known about the situation. However, she allowed me to stay anyway because she silently supported me, regardless of what my mother and Mr. Abdul were saying. To Rebbie, I was family, but more importantly a college student and she wanted to show support for my choice to at least continue my education. My mother would never come to speak to me as her daughter. She periodically told me that she loved me, but I never felt the love or witnessed the love through her actions; instead I felt betrayed. Weeks went by and realizing that I was determined not to return home, Rebbie made arrangements for my return back to college and eventually made me a permanent member of her family.

For a few years my mother and her new husband would periodically go and meet with Rebbie accusing her of "stealing her daughter" and not supporting their choice of discipline, but regardless of the controversy Rebbie would never agree per their request to make me leave; at not least at that point.

My mother then began stopping all communication between my siblings and I. She even went as far as advising my siblings that they were NOT to speak to me. If they were found to have contacted me, they would be faced with being disciplined and that it would be severe. I was labeled by my mother and Mr. Abdul as a "bad influence" and this time they had evidence, as I'd blatantly disregarded their years of requests for me to return home and comply with their rules.

During this period the pressure of being the big sister, the savior, the good example, the supporter, was conflicting in both my head as well as in my siblings. At times I would miss them so much I couldn't stand it anymore, so I'd go to my mother's apartment just so I could see my sisters . She wouldn't allow me in her apartment but she would allow me to stand at the screen door and speak with them through the screen. That didn't matter to me though, because at least I could see them.

As time went on my sisters began contacting me secretly and even worst, their phone calls were mostly tear-filled. They would tell me about all of the horrible things that Mr. Abdul would do to them and with my mother's blessings; as my mother would relentlessly remind them Mr. Abdul came first in their home, as it was written in the bible.

Some of the things they reported were very strange like when Mr. Abdul came home from work, if my siblings were watching TV, he'd walk in and change the channel. Our mother wanted them to call him Daddy and that it was directed to them with her infamous "or else clause." He was to be served the last portion of food, even if they hadn't eaten because he's her "husband and sole provider in the home," thus he must eat before anyone.

As one might expect, as my sisters grew older they begin to lash out, as most teenagers' wanting more freedom, normally do. They wanted fair treatment along with some support and relief from our Mother. Many times Mr. Abdul found them deserving of being disciplined severely as a way to get back at them; all with my mother's faithful support.

I was paralyzed with grief and shocked as each year one of my siblings behaviors would eventually get so out of hand because the ill-treatment in the home. Coupled with Mr. Abdul's silent retaliatory acts, and our mother always siding with him because he was her husband; always lead up to one of my sisters being put out with no plan for their care. Group homes, boyfriend's homes and jail were places my siblings went because they were too young to support themselves. The reports from my siblings stressed me out and depressed me all at the same time because there was nothing I could do to help them. So, I did the only thing I could do- provide them with advise, loyalty, love, distant support and an always open ear to listen to their troubles.

After completing my associate's degree in upstate Connecticut, I was recruited heavily from all across the country by colleges and university basketball teams wanting me to play for their teams. I chose to stay in the tri-state area because I didn't want to be too far from my sisters. With no guidance or adult support, I obtained a full athletic scholarship to a university, playing D1 basketball. I still have my offer letter and on the line where a parents' signature is required, there is none.

As a full-time student athlete at the Iona College, I endured many silent, tear filled breakdowns in my dorm room alone. I would never be able to tell anyone my troubles because no one could either relate to or understand. I'd get frustrated while explaining the situation. Most people didn't believe me and felt I was exaggerating my experiences.

As anyone could imagine it was very hard to concentrate on maintaining a reputable GPA and I was reduced to viewing basketball as a job. I played to ensure that I had a place to live, so that way I wasn't at Rebbie's house year round.

At Rebbie's house I had a lot more freedom. I was allowed to be a young adult, but more importantly I was allowed to party with her daughter, Vanessa. Vanessa was a few years older than me and loved going out to Jamaican clubs. But in order to get me to join her at those types of clubs she would 1st have to agree to take me to an American club for a few hours.

One night I was out with Vanessa at a Jamaican club (I was not too excited about that), but was still enjoying my freedom to party. And in walks Daytron, a Jamaican man a little taller than me; brown skinned, with long eyelashes, tapped me on my shoulder and asked me for a dance. He paid so much attention to me; I lost all focus about my life, my problems, and my goals.

We eventually would fall madly in love; a match made in heaven so I thought. Daytron was a low level drug dealer. He too was homeless but that was because his middle class Jamaican family grew tired of his failure to, "Mek sup'm outta 'im life," so they put him out. Daytron didn't seem to be troubled by his living arrangements so he gave me strength to not worry too much about my own situation. He sold drugs and made enough money to feed us; enough to get a party outfit here and there and pay our way into various parties.

I began to spend every weekend with Daytron. And being young and very inexperienced with boys, I eventually became pregnant. The 1st time I got pregnant we decided that I was a college student and that I should stay focused and complete my education, so we decided not to keep the baby. With all of the trauma I'd already been through, this decision only exaggerated and intensified my depression as it added a thick layer of guilt. Daytron had also been affected. He cried the day we went to terminate the pregnancy.

So, armed with birth control pills and a young, forgetful mind, I went on with my life. I got pregnant again within 3 months post abortion but this time I kept it. During one of my breaks I went home and told Vanessa, as I knew she'd been in my shoes several times before and assured me that it wasn't a big deal. I told her I wasn't ready to tell anyone and to please keep my pregnancy a secret until I built enough strength to tell them myself.

So the very next day at breakfast, Rebbie said to me so, "Danni you're pregnant now. Where are you going to live"? On that day I became a pregnant college student who was now homeless for the second time.

Author's Note

As a child and young adult I found my life at times consumed with "trying to get it right" in order to "fit in" with my birth family. I eventually had to take on a mindset that required me to first, give myself permission to receive peace; as peace had been stripped from me for such a large part of my life. Some of those things included self initiated separation, addressing and standing firm when confronting incidents that involve ill treatment, while I continued to profess innate true feelings of love for my family, despite of what's said because God knows my heart.

I did not, nor could I have chosen my birth family. My family is my birth right and I endured many years of traumatic experiences; leaving me as an outsider (not to all but to many) because I chose to eventually speak up. I've written about my experience, not to hurt my family, but to show the various ways in which one can survive in spite of years of intensive emotional abuse, abandonment and rejection from those whom most consider the most important people in their lives; their family.

It saddens me when people question my love for my family, because that's all that I have ever had for them and all I ever wanted from them. Yes, I've been hurt. Yet God placed this deep desire within me to have me reveal my hurts and struggles, in hopes that people recognize the significant healing processes which took place. For even when I'd just about given up, God sent angels. He had a plan for my life.

At times, this story was EXTREMELY hard to write; as I had to relive all that I've gone through as a child and as a young adult. However, I also acknowledge that these experiences are what have made me into the strong and loving woman that I am today.

My desire for people who chose to read my book is that its contents are utilized in ways, in which to help girls, boys, men and women, who've like myself have struggled with finding their way in life without a loving and supportive mother and family. Most importantly, my hope is that my words inspire people to seek help when they find themselves in need emotionally.

My prayer is that people seek God first and find a way in which to accept love and support replacement for mothers, fathers and families to help make them whole. For those individuals who have troubled relationships with their mother and who question whether their needs for motherly love and support will ever be met; I leave you with this scripture, "And my God I will meet all your needs in according to his riches in Jesus Christ" ~ Philippians 4:19.